S T A T E   P U B L

/ORCESTER

ROITWICH   GREAT MALVERN

C000015801

Claines
4

Fernhill
Heath
5

10
Warndon

Lower
Broadheath
6   7

8 Ronkswood
3   9

Dines Green

WORCESTER   11 Spetchley

St. Johns
12   13

Cherry
Orchard
14   15

Rushwick

Whittington

Powick

16
Callow End

17
Kempsey

Malvern
Link
18   19

West Malvern   GREAT MALVERN

Poolbrook
20   21

Upper Colwall

Colwall Stone
22   23

Malvern Wells

ROAD MAP   Page 2
ENLARGED CENTRE   Page 3
INDEX TO STREETS   Page 26

Car Park	🅿
Public Convenience	🅒
Place of Worship	+
One-Way Street	→
Pedestrianized	▨
Post Office	●

Scale of street plans 4 inches to 1 mile
Unless otherwise stated

Street plans prepared and published by ESTATE PUBLICATIONS, Bridewell House,
TENTERDEN, KENT, and based upon the ORDNANCE SURVEY mapping with the permission
of The Controller of H. M. Stationery Office.

The Publishers acknowledge the co-operation of the local authorities
of towns represented in this atlas.

State Publications 567 A   ISBN 0 86084 792 6   © Crown Copyright 398713

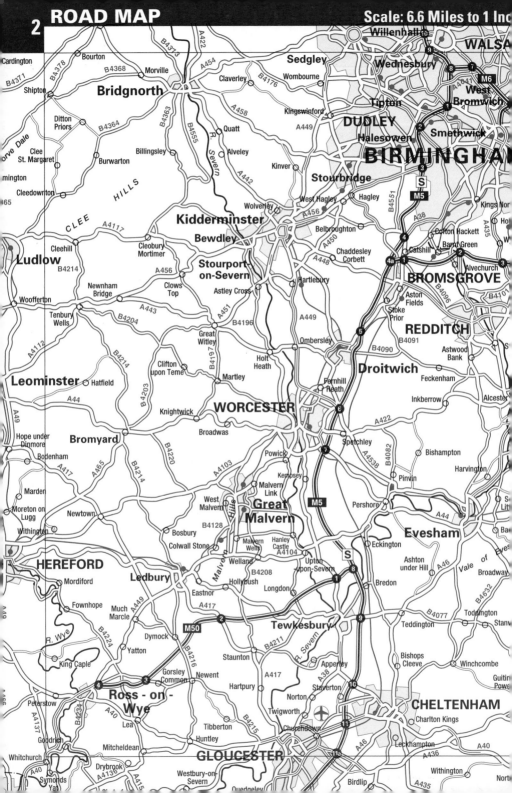

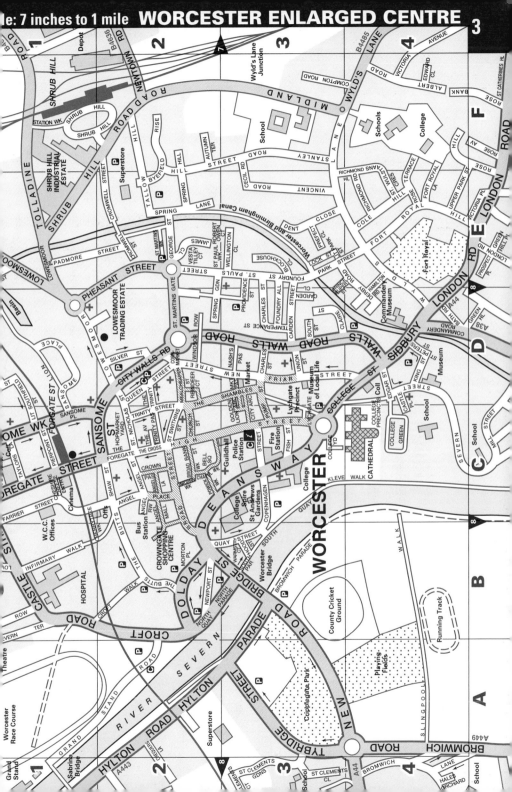

Lower Town, Martin's Court Farm, Martin Hussingtree, Martin Brook, Tapenhall Farm, Fernhill Heath, Post Office, School, Hindlip, Cricket Ground, Hindlip Hall Police H.Q., Farm Plantation, The Crescent, Court Farm, Police Station, High Wood, Moathouse Farm, Barbourne Brook, Blackpole Trading Estate West, Blackpole Trading Estate East, Spellis Grn, Spring Bank, Cricket Ground, Blackpole, Worcester & Birmingham Canal, Buckholt Business Park, Warndon Business Park, Tolladine Lock, Shire Business Park, Depot, Industrial Estate, Cranham, Elgar Retail Park, Sports Ground, Astwood, School, Playing Field, Liby, Berkeley, Woodgreen Drive.

Road and street labels include:
DANES GREEN, DILMORE LANE, MORTON ROAD, MORTON AV, TAPENHALL ROAD, DILMORE RD, DILMORE AV, CRESSWELL, NORTHFIELD, WESTFIELD, SHRAWLEY, BROADFIELD CRES, BROOM MDW, EASTFIELD, BROADFIELD CRES, ASCOT CL, EPSOM CL, PERRY CROFT, STATION ROAD, WILLOW ROAD, FIR TREE, PINE TREE, OKEYS LA, IVY LA, DROITWICH ROAD, HURST LANE, A4536, B4550, ROAD, HINDLIP LANE, THE DRIVE, THE CRESCENT, DRIVE, A449, A38, KENNELS LANE, THE DERRIES, SLING LANE, OLD, B4639, COTSWOLD, CRANHAM DR, BUCKHOLT DRIVE, PRESCOTT DRIVE, BADGEWORTH, WAINWRIGHT, EBRINGTON, ROAD, WAINW, GRESLEY RD, STANIER RD, BLAIR, WAY, BRINDLE, BERKEL, HASTINGS, WINDERMERE DRIVE, BLACKPOLE RD, KERRY HILL, SUFFOLK WAY, COSGROVE, WENSLEY, RYLAND, DROVERS WAY, BILFORD ROAD, FARM CLOSE, PINE, MASONS, TANNERS, TURNERS, CARTERS, VINTNERS, JOINERS, WINCHCOMBE DRIVE, LYE HAM, COLESBORNE, ELKSTONE, HAMPTON, AMBERLEY CL, STANWAY CL, NIBLEY, RANDWICK DR, RAVENING CL, HARESFIELD, BISLEY, WITNEY CT, COBERLEY, SHEEPSCOMBE, CHEDWORTH, CRICKLEY, SELSEY, SNOWSHILL, OAKRIDGE, DALEGARTH CT, LINLEY, SWALEDALE, WASDALE, BEARCROFT, LEWES GDNS, BODIAM, LUDLOW, CASTLE, HONISTER, HAWKES, SHAP, BURFORD, RODBOROUGH, BROOKTHORPE DR, CHATCOMBE DR, LECKHAMPTON, PAINSWICK, CHEDWORTH, WOODGREEN DRIVE, MARTLEY.

Grid references E, F, G, H across the top and 1, 2, 3, 4, 5, 6 down the right side.

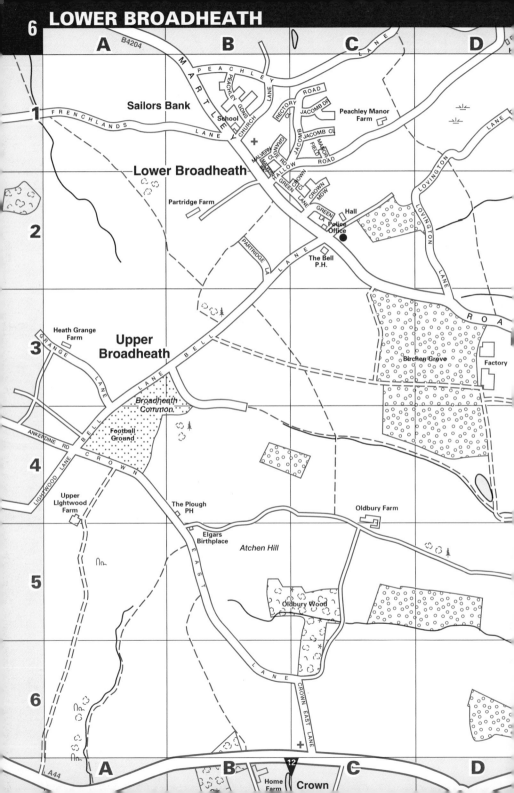

A · B · C · D

B4204

Sailors Bank

PEACHLEY LANE

MARTLEY LANE

School

CHURCH

RECTORY CL

ROAD

JACOMB DR

JACOMB CL

Peachley Manor Farm

MANOR FIELD

ROAD

Lower Broadheath

1

MALVERN CL

CLOSE

BROAD

HALLOW

GREEN

CLOSE

CROWN

LANE

GREEN LA

Hall

Police Office

Partridge Farm

PARTRIDGE LA

LANE

The Bell P.H.

2

LOVINGTON LANE

ROAD

Heath Grange Farm

GRANGE LANE

Upper Broadheath

BELL LANE

Birchen Grove

Factory

3

Broadheath Common

Football Ground

ANKERDINE RD

LIGHTWOOD LANE

BELL

CROWN

4

Upper Lightwood Farm

The Plough PH

Elgars Birthplace

EAST

Atchen Hill

Oldbury Farm

5

Oldbury Wood

LANE

6

CROWN EAST LANE

A44

A · B · **12** · C · D

Home Farm

Crown

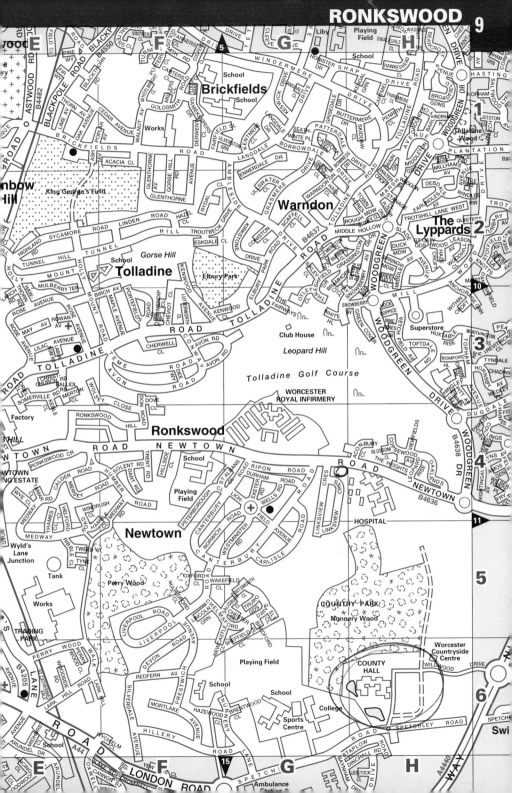

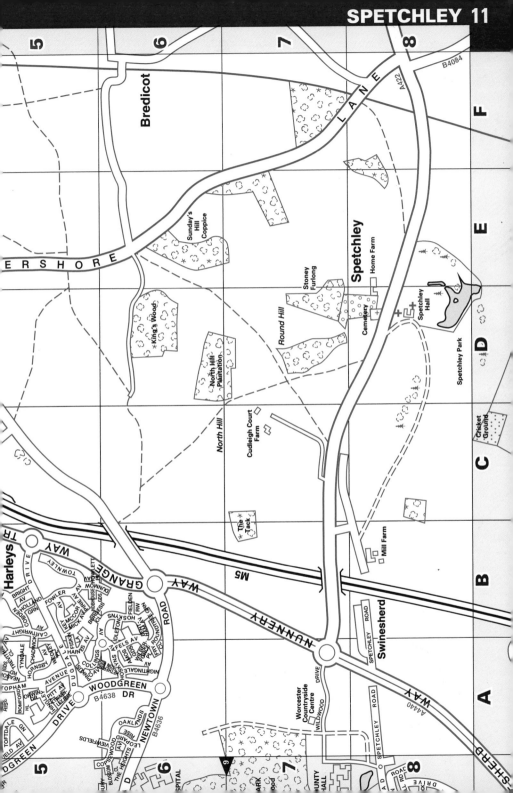

5 6 7 8

B4084

A422

F

Bredicot

E

PERSHORE

Sunday's Hill Coppice

Spetchley

Home Farm

Stoney Furlong

Cemetery

Spetchley Hall

King's Wood

Round Hill

Spetchley Park

D

North Hill Plantation

North Hill

Cudleigh Court Farm

Cricket Ground

C

The Jack

Mill Farm

Harleys Tr

GRANGE WAY

M5

ROAD WAY

NUNNERY WAY

Swinesherd ROAD

SPETCHLEY ROAD

B

A4440 WAY

A

WOODGREEN DR

B4638

NEWTOWN

B4636

Worcester Countryside Centre

WILDWOOD DRIVE

COUNTY HALL

SWINESHER'D

5 6 7 8

DRIVE RD

A422

A44

LANE
OTHERTON LANE
OTHERTON LANE

Grove
Covert

Home
Farm

Crown
East

School

Otherton
Farm

Rushwick

GROVE A4440

CLAPHILL LANE

BROADMORE GN

CORONATION AV
GRANGE LA
ORCHARD CL
MINETT AV
WHITEHALL CL
VIVIAN AV
CHRISTINE AV
AVENUE

Cricket
Ground

Bransford
Bridge

A4103

River Teme

Ten Ho
Farm

Bransford
Court

Foxholes Wood

Lords Wood

Whitegate
Farm

Midleyard
Coppice

Dawshill

KINGS END
HAM

16

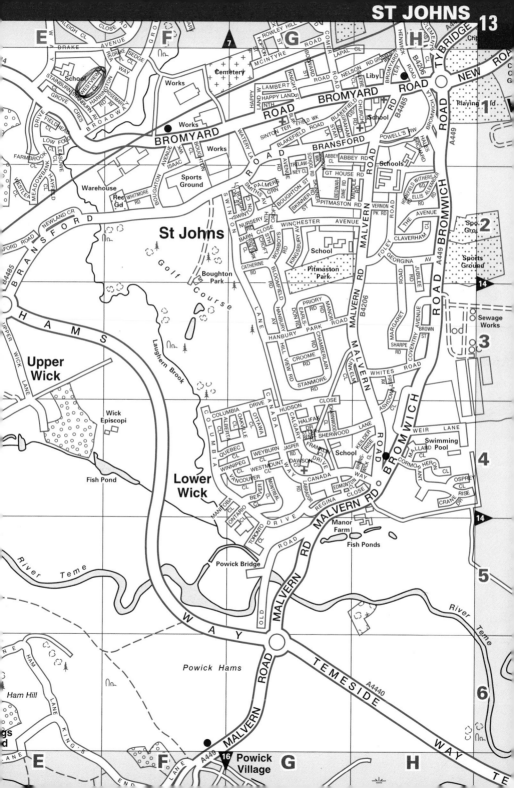

St Johns

Upper Wick

Lower Wick

Wick Episcopi

Fish Pond

Golf Course

Boughton Park

Pitmaston Park

Swimming Pool

Sewage Works

Sports Ground

Powick Hams

Ham Hill

River Teme

River Teme

Laughern Brook

Powick Bridge

Manor Farm

Fish Ponds

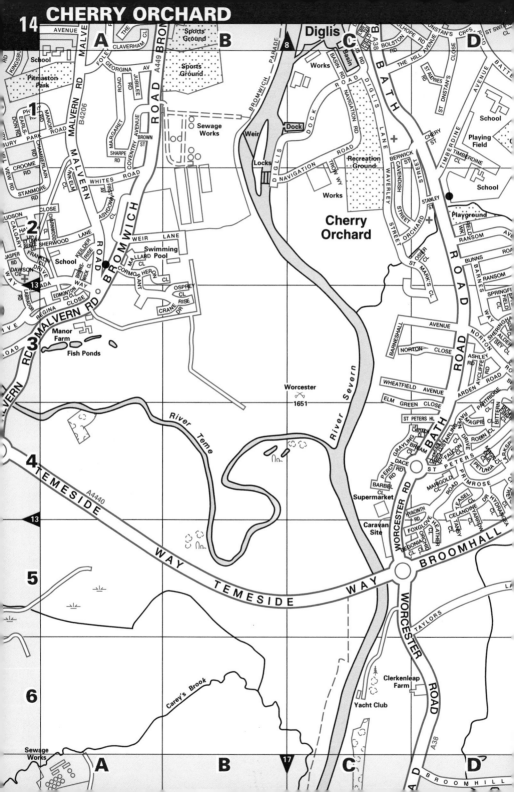

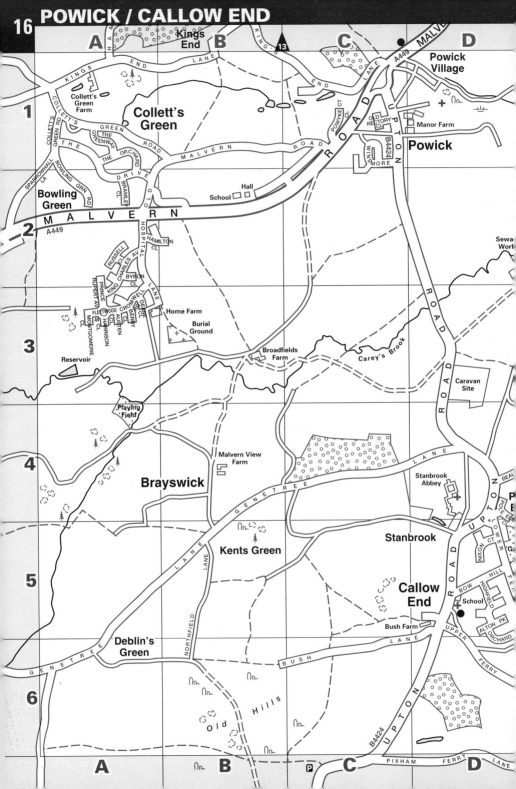

Kings End

Collett's Green

Collett's Green Farm

Bowling Green

Powick Village

Powick

Manor Farm

Old Rectory Cl

School

Hall

MALVERN A449

Hamilton Cl

Russell Cl

King Charles Av

Byron Cl

Prince Rupert Av

Fleetwood Av

Montgomerie Cl

Harrison

Austen

Cromwell Drive

Berry

Home Farm

Burial Ground

Reservoir

Broadfields Farm

Carey's Brook

Caravan Site

Playing Field

Malvern View Farm

Brayswick

Stanbrook Abbey

Stanbrook

Kents Green

Callow End

School

Genetree Lane

Northfield Lane

Deblin's Green

Bush Farm

Bush Lane

Upper Ferry Lane

Upton Road

Bow Hill

Highfield

Alton Pk

Orchard

Old Hills

Genetree Lane

Pixham Ferry Lane

B4424 Upton

Sewage Works

E · F · G · H

BROOMHILL LANE

Lower Broomhall Farm

Holdings Farm

1

HOLDINGS

HOLDINGS LANE

Beauchamp Court

BEAUCHAMP LA

Upper Ham

2

RIVER SEVERN

Kempsey Grove

A38 ROAD

WORCESTER ROAD

KINGS HILL

WINDMILL LANE

Police Station

School

HILLSIDE

THE LIMES

THE LIMES

LANE

Brookend Farm

Brook End

3

BROOKEND

BROOK SIDE

BROOK CL

Caravan Park

ROOKERY RD

COURT MDW

COURT GARTH

LANE'S END

CHAPEL LANE

HETHERINGTON CL

ANSTY CL

LYTTS LANE

ST MARYS CL

CHURCH STREET

ROAD NORTH

OLD ROAD

Hatfield Brook

Kempsey

LANE

4

School

ELLSDON

ELLSDON RISE

POST OFFICE

DRIVE

OAKFIELD

SQUIRE'S CL

SQUIRE'S WALK

SOUTH ROAD

WORCESTER ROAD

THE FREELANDS

OLD VICARAGE CL

ELGAR DR

NAPLETON

FLORENCE CL

DARWIN

PLOVERS RISE

ADELAIDE CL

FREEMANTLE DR

Bannut Hill

LANE

NAPLETON LANE

Napleton

5

Lower Ham

PIXHAM FERRY LA

PIXHAM FERRY LANE

OLD ROAD

A38 ROAD

BESTMANS LANE

LANE

M5

6

E · F · G · H

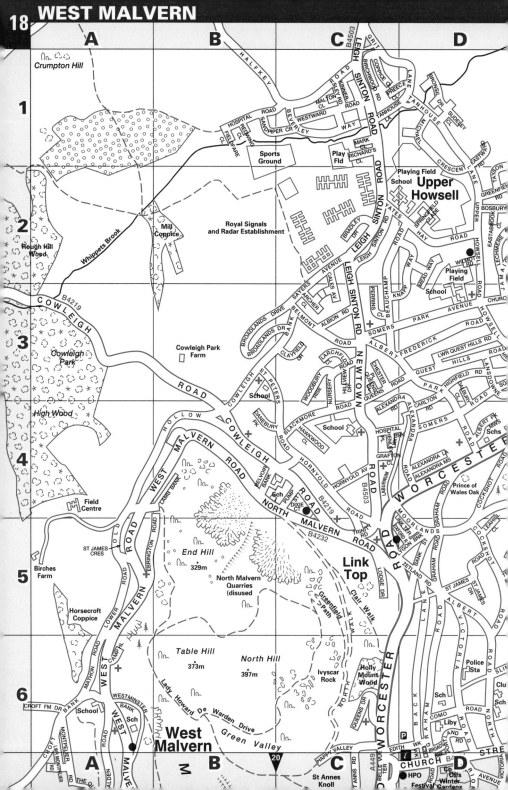

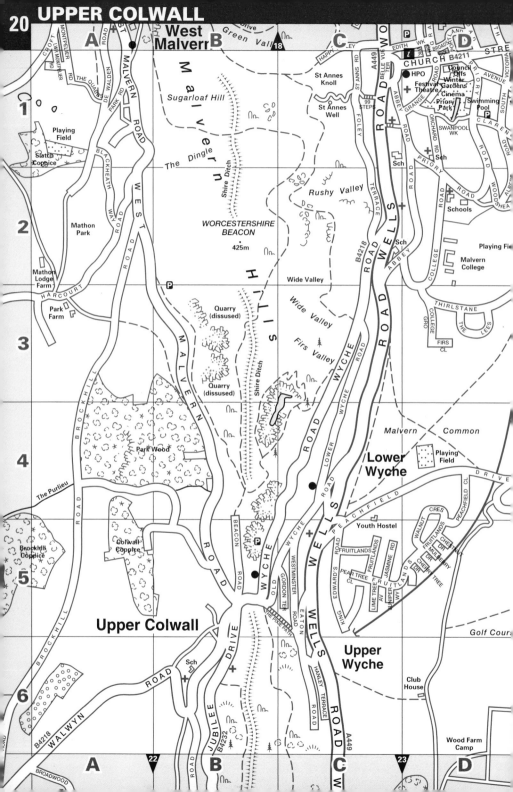

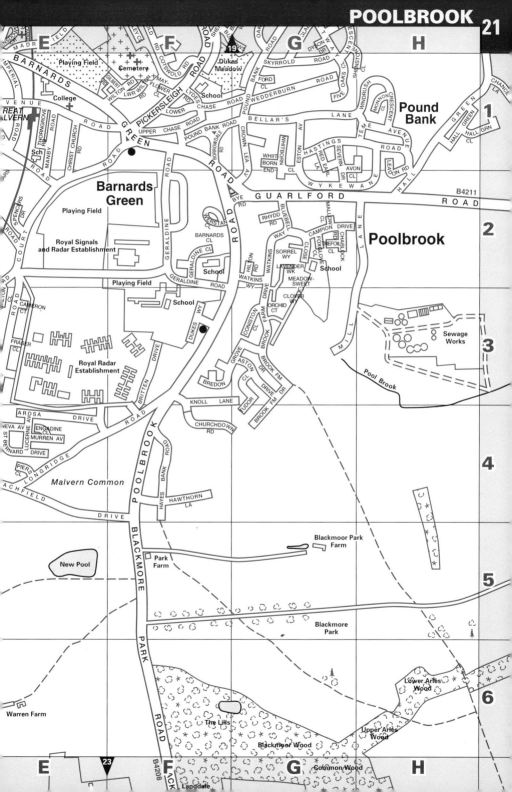

Playing Field
Cemetery
College
Sch
VENUE
GREAT MALVERN
THORNGROVE ROAD
MANBY RD
CHRIST CHURCH RD
IMPERIAL ROAD
BARNARDS
Dukes Meadow
School
COTSWOLD RD
SHELLEY CL
ROAD
PICKERSLEIGH
GREEN
ROAD
LWR WILTON RD
WILTON RD
GILBERTS RD
MAY-FLOWER CL
LYDES RD
UPPER CHASE ROAD
LOWER CHASE ROAD
POUND BANK ROAD
BORROWDALE RD
CROWN LEA AV

SKYRROLD ROAD
OAKS CL
FORD CL
WEDDERBURN
FIVE OAKS CL
POUND BANK
BELLAR'S LANE
WINDRUSH
MONKWOOD CRESCENT
CRESCENT
AVENUE
TEME AV
Pound
Bank
CHANGE LA
HALL GREEN
HALL GREEN CL
GRN

Barnards Green

Playing Field

Royal Signals
and Radar Establishment

Playing Field

School

**Royal Radar
Establishment**

GERALDINE DRIVE
GERALDINE CL
GERALDINE ROAD
DUKES WY

BRITTEN ROAD

AROSA DRIVE
GENEVA AV
ENGADINE CL
LUCERNE AV
MURREN AV
ST BERNARD DRIVE
PIERS CL
ACHFIELD
LONGRIDGE

FRASER CL
CAMERON CT
SPENCERS DR
COURT

WEBSTAN
BARNARDS CL
GERALDINE CL
School
School

HILTON RD
WATKINS WY
WATKINS WY

CONISTON CL
GROVE
BROOK FM DR
ASTON DR
BREDON
KNOLL LANE
TUDOR CL
CHURCHDOWN RD

WHITBORN CL
ESTON AV
HASTINGS
CROWN END
WHITT-BORN CL
RED EARL DR
AVON CL

RHYDD RD
BLUEBELL RD
WAY
SORREL WY
LAVENDER WK
MEADOW-SWEET
CLOVER WY
ORCHID CT

MALLOW RD
CAMPION DRIVE
TREFOIL CL
FOXGLOVE
CLOSE
CHARLOCK CL
School

SEVERN DR
LEADON RD
WYKE WANE
HALL

GUARLFORD ROAD
B4211
ROAD

Poolbrook

MILL LANE
Sewage Works

Pool Brook

POOLBROOK ROAD
HAYES BANK ROAD
HAWTHORN LA
DRIVE

BLACKMORE PARK ROAD

Malvern Common

New Pool

Park Farm

Blackmoor Park Farm

Blackmore Park

Warren Farm

Lower Arles Wood

Upper Arles Wood

The Lills

Blackmoor Wood

Common Wood

Langdale

B4208
JACK

Colwall
Stone

COLWALL

Grovesend
Farm

Cricket
Field

School

Liby

Cheverham

Brookside

Cricket
Ground

Swimming
Pool

School

School

Evendine
Corner

Evendine

Brand Green

Baxhill
Coppice

Pen
Coppice

Gardeners
Common

Hanway's
Coppice

Perry
Croft
Coppice

Hawketts
Coppice

Swinepits
Coppice

Woodlands
Coppice

Herrings Coppice

Fish
Pond

Old Castle
Farm

Fishpool
Lays Coppice

Wynds
Point

Black Hill

The
Grove

Hatfield
Coppice

Herefordshire
Beacon

Tinkers Hill

E A449 20 F ood Farm Camp G 21 H BLACKMORE PARK ROAD

Hills

Langdale Wood

Hornyold Wood

WELLS ROAD

HOLY WELL

BENBOW CL.

B4209

HANLEY ROAD

WOOD FARM ROAD

Sports Field Sports Ground

Cricket Ground

THREE COUNTIES SHOWGROUND

1

Malvern Wells

THE MOORLANDS

GRUNDY'S LA.

School

B4209

ROAD B4208

2

GREEN LANE HANLEY ROAD

OAKLANDS

ROTHWELL RD

Cemetery Playing Field

Brickbarns Farm

SHUTTLEFAST LANE

3

Pol Sta

Shuttlefast Farm

Malvern

HOLY WELL ROAD

ROAD

The Abbey

School

CRESCENT

St PETERS CL

THE

St WULSTANS

BLACKHILL

MEREBROOK DRIVE

4

ASSARTS

WELLS

HEATHLANDS CL

UPPER

ROAD

ASSARTS

WELLAND

Play. Fld

YEW TREE LA.

CHASE ROAD

CAMBRIDGE CL.

Mere Brook

Playing Field

Upper Welland

Elgars Grave (Site of)

KINGS ROAD

WELLS

Woodend Farm

Wood Farm

5

North Farm

Little Malvern

A4104

WATERY LANE

ROAD

Mayalls Farm

Days Farm

Priory Benedictine (founded 1171)

6

A4104

Yew Tree Farm

HANCOCKS LA.

E F G H

The Index includes some names for which there is insufficient space on the maps. These names are preceded by an * and are followed by the nearest adjoining thoroughfare.

DROITWICH

Lower Rd WR14 18 A5
Lower Wilton Rd WR14 21 F1
Lower Wyche Rd WR14 20 C4
Lucerne Av WR14 21 E4
Lydes Rd WR14 21 F1
Lygon Bank WR14 18 D5

Macauley Rise WR14 19 E4
Madresfield Rd WR14 19 E6
Mallow Cl WR14 21 G2
Malton Cl WR14 18 C1
Malus Cl WR14 19 G4
Manby Rd WR14 21 E1
Mansfield Way WR14 19 G4
Mark Cl WR14 18 C1
Marlborough Gdns WR14 19 E1
Marsh Cl WR14 19 F5
Martins Orchard WR13 22 A3
Mason Cl WR14 19 F4
Mathon Rd WR14 18 A6
Mathon Rd, Colwall WR14 22 B1
Matravers Rd WR14 19 F5
May Bank WR14 19 F4
Mayfield Rd WR14 19 G6
Mayflower Cl WR14 21 F1
Meadow Rd WR14 19 E4
Meadowsweet Ct WR14 21 G3
Meadow Walk WR13 22 B1
Mead Way WR14 18 D2
Mendip Cl WR14 19 F6
Merebrook Cl WR13 23 F4
Merick Rd WR14 19 F2
Merton Rd WR14 19 E3
Michael Cres WR14 18 D1
Mill La, Colwall WR13 22 A2
Mill La WR14 21 G3
Moat Cres WR14 19 G6
Moatway WR14 19 G6
Monnon Cl WR14 21 H1
Montpelier Rd WR14 18 A6
Moorlands Rd WR14 18 D4
Mountbatten Rd WR14 19 G5
Mulberry Dr WR14 20 D5
Murren Av WR14 21 E4

New Ct WR13 22 B1
Newtown Rd WR14 18 C3
Nightingale Rd WR14 19 G5
North End La WR14 19 F5
North Malvern Rd WR14 18 B4
Nursery Rd WR14 18 C3

Oak Cres WR14 19 G6
Oak Dr WR13 22 B1
Oakfield Rd WR14 19 E2
Oaklands WR14 23 F2
Old Hollow WR14 18 A5
Old Orchard Rd WR13 22 A1
Old Wyche Rd WR14 20 B5
Orchard Rd WR14 19 E2
Orchid Ct WR14 21 G3
Orford Way WR14 19 F5
Orlin Rd WR13 22 A1
Oxford Rd WR14 18 C5

Park Cl WR14 19 F3
Park Rd WR14 20 A1
Parkside WR13 22 B2
Peachfield Cl WR14 20 D4
Peachfield Dr WR14 20 C5
Pear Tree Cl WR14 20 C5
Percy Walton Cl WR14 21 E3
Perrins Cl WR14 18 C3
Pickersleigh Av WR14 19 E3
Pickersleigh Cl WR14 19 E3
Pickersleigh Gro WR14 19 E5
Pickersleigh Rd WR14 19 E3
Piers Cl WR14 21 E4
Players Av WR14 19 E2
Poolbrook Rd WR14 21 F4
Portland Rd WR14 18 D6
Pound Bank Rd WR14 21 F1
Princess Margaret Av WR14 19 F2
Priory Rd WR14 20 D1
Pump St WR14 18 C4

Queen Elizabeth Rd WR14 19 F2
Queens Cl WR14 18 C3
Queens Dr WR14 18 C6
Queens Rd WR14 18 C3
Quest Hills Rd WR14 18 D3

Ramsons Cl WR14 19 F4
Ranelagh Rd WR14 19 F2
Rectory La WR14 19 H4
Red Earl La WR14 21 G1
Redland Cl WR14 19 E2
Redland Rd WR14 19 E3
Redlingham Cl WR13 22 B1
Redwing Cl WR14 18 B1
Regency Rd WR14 19 F2
Rhydd Rd WR14 21 G2
Richards Cl WR14 18 C1
Richmond Rd WR14 19 E3
Roman Way WR14 19 G2
Rothwell Rd WR14 23 F2
Russell Dr WR14 19 E3

St Andrews Rd WR14 21 E4
St Anns Rd WR14 20 C1
St Bernard Dr WR14 21 E4
St James Cres WR14 18 A5
St James Dr WR14 18 D5
St James Rd WR14 18 D5
St Peters Cl WR13 23 F4
St Peters Rd WR14 18 B3
St Wulstans Dr WR13 23 F4
Sandpiper Cres WR14 18 B1
Sandringham Cl WR14 19 G1
Sandys Rd WR14 19 G4
Sayers Av WR14 18 C3
Severn Dr WR14 21 G1
Shaw Walk WR14 19 G5
Shenstone Cl WR14 21 G1
Sherrards Green Rd WR14 19 F6
Shirley Cl WR14 19 F6
Shuttlefast La WR14 23 G2
Silver St WR13 22 B1
Skyrrold Rd WR14 21 G1
Sling La WR14 18 D6
Somer Rd WR14 18 D4
Somers Park Av WR14 18 C3
Sorrel Way WR14 21 G2
Spencers Dr WR14 21 E2
Spencers Way WR14 19 F2
Spindle Rd WR14 19 G4
Spring Cl WR13 22 B1
Springfield Glade WR14 18 D2
Spring Gdns WR14 19 F2
Spring La WR14 19 F3
Spring La North WR14 19 F3
Spring La South WR14 19 F3
Stanley Rd WR14 19 E6
Steamer Point WR14 19 F5
Stone Cl WR13 22 A1
Stone Ct WR13 22 B1
Stone Dr WR13 22 B1
Stowe La WR13 22 A3
Sudeley Cl WR14 18 D1
Summerfield Rd WR14 19 E2
Sunrise WR14 19 F6
Swanpool Walk WR14 20 D1
Sycamore Cl WR14 19 E1

Tanhouse La WR14 18 C1
Tayson Way WR14 18 D2
Teme Av WR14 21 H1
Tennyson Dr WR14 18 D5
The Crescent, Colwall WR13 22 A2
The Crescent, Welland WR14 23 F4
The Glade WR14 19 G6
The Lees WR14 20 D3
The Moorlands WR14 23 F2
The Quabbs WR14 20 A1
Thirlstane Rd WR14 20 D3
Thorngrove Rd WR14 21 E1
Tibberton Rd WR14 21 E1
Townsend Way WR14 19 G2
Trefoil Cl WR14 21 G2
Trinity Rd WR14 18 C5
Tudor Rd WR14 21 G4

Upper Chase Rd WR14 21 F1
Upper Ct WR13 22 B1
Upper Howsell Rd WR14 18 D2
Upper Welland Rd WR14 23 E4

Vandra Cl WR14 19 F1
Victoria Park Rd WR14 19 E3
Victoria Rd WR14 18 D5
Victoria Rd WR14 20 D1

Walnut Cres WR14 20 D5
Walwyn Rd WR13 20 A6
Watery La WR14 23 F6
Watkins Way WR14 21 G2
Wedderburn Rd 14 21 G1
Wells Cl WR14 23 E4
Wells Rd WR14 20 C2
Werstan Cl WR14 21 F2
West Malvern Rd WR14 18 A6
Westlyn Cl WR14 19 E4
Westminster Bank WR14 18 A6
Westminster Rd WR14 20 C5
Westward Rd WR14 18 C1
Whitborn Cl WR14 21 G1
Whitborn End WR14 21 G1
Whitethorn Gro WR14 19 G4
Willow Gro WR14 19 E4
Wilmot Rd WR14 18 D2
Wilton Rd WR14 21 F1
Windrush Cres WR14 21 H1
Windsor Cl WR14 19 G1
Woodbury Rise WR14 18 C3
Wood Farm Rd WR14 23 E1
Woodlands WR13 23 E4
Woodshears Dr WR14 21 E2
Woodshears Rd WR14 20 D2
Worcester Rd WR14 18 D4
Wren Av WR14 19 G5
Wyche Rd WR14 20 C3
Wykewane WR14 21 G2

Yates Hay Rd WR14 18 C2
Yew Tree Cl WR13 22 A4
Yew Tree La WR14 23 F4
York Cl WR14 19 F1

Zetland Rd WR14 18 D5

WORCESTER

Abbey Cl WR2 13 G1
Abbey Rd WR2 13 G1
Abbotsbury Ct WR5 15 E3
Abbots Cl WR4 7 F5
Acacia Cl WR4 9 F1
Aconbury Cl WR5 9 H4
Addison Rd WR3 4 C6
Admiral Pl WR5 15 F4
Albany Rd WR3 8 D2
Albany Ter WR1 8 B3
Alberta Cl WR4 13 F4
Albert Rd WR5 3 F4
Alder Cl WR3 9 E2
Aldersey Cl WR5 14 D3
Alexander Rd WR2 13 H2
Alma St WR3 4 C6
Alton Park WR2 16 D5
Amberley Cl WR4 5 F6
Ambleside Dr WR4 9 G1
Ambrose Cl WR2 7 E5
Amery Cl WR5 15 E1
Amos Gdns WR4 11 A6
Amroth Cl WR4 10 A2
Anchorage Grn WR4 9 H3
Andrew Cl WR2 7 F5
Angel La WR1 3 C2
Angel Mall WR1 3 C2
Angel Pl WR1 3 C2
Angel Row WR1 3 C2
Angel St WR1 3 C2
Arboretum Rd WR1 8 C3
Arden Rd WR5 14 D3
Arran Pl WR5 15 F3
Arrowsmith Av WR2 7 H6
Ascot Cl WR3 5 F2
Ash Av WR4 9 E1

Ashcroft Rd WR1 8
Ashdown Cl WR2 13
Ashley Rd WR5 14
Astwood Rd WR3 5
Athelstan Rd WR5 8
Austen Cl WR2 16
Autumn Ter WR5 3
Avening Cl WR3 5
Avenue Rd WR2 13
Avon Rd WR4 9
Aycliffe Rd WR5 14

Bacchurst Pl WR4 10
Back La North WR 8
Back La South WR1 8
Badger Gdns WR5 15
Badgeworth Dr WR 8
*Baffin Rd, Edmonton Cl WR2 13
Bala Way WR5 15
Balliol Rd WR4 9
Bamburgh Cres WR4 10
Bankside Cl WR3 4
Bank St WR1 3
Bannut Hill WR5 17
Barass Av WR4 10
Barbel Cl WR5 14
Barbers Cl WR4 5
Barbourne Cres WR1 8
Barbourne La WR1 8
Barbourne Rd WR1 8
Barbourne Ter WR1 8
Barbourne Walk WR1 8
Barker St WR3 8
Barley Cres WR4 9
Barn Cl WR2 13
Barneshall Av WR5 14
Barnes Way WR5 14
Barry St WR1 8
Basin Rd WR5 14
Bath Rd WR5 8
Batsford Rd 15
Battenhall Av WR5 15
Battenhall Pl WR5 8
Battenhall Rd WR5 8
Battenhall Rise WR5 15
Battenhall Walk WR5 8
Battle Rd WR5 15
Baveney Rd WR2 7
Baynham Dr WR5 15
Beaconhill Dr WR2 7
Bearcroft Av WR4 10
Beauchamp La WR2 16
Beaver Cl WR2 13
Beckett Cl WR3 4
Beckett Dr WR3 4
Beckett Rd WR3 4
Bedwardine Rd WR2 13
Beech Av WR3 4
Beech Av North WR3 4
Beeston Gdns WR4 10
Begonia Cl WR5 14
Bell La WR2 6
Belmont St WR3 8
Bell Square WR1 3
Bentham Av WR4 11
Berkeley Cl WR5 15
Berkeley St WR1 8
Berry Cl WR2 16
Berwick St WR5 14
Bestmans La WR5 17
Bevere Cl WR3 4
Bevere Cl South WR3 4
Bevere Ct WR3 4
Bevere Dr WR3 4
Bevere La WR3 4
Bicton Av WR5 15
Bicton Av North WR5 5
Bilford Av WR3 5
Bilford Rd WR3 4
Birchangel Grn WR4 10
Birch Av WR4 9
Birchfield Cl WR3 4
Birdlip Cl WR4 5
Bishops Av WR5 8
Bisley Cl WR4 5
Bittern Rd WR5 14
Blackpole Rd WR3 WR4 5

ckthorn Rd WR4 9 E1
agdon Cl WR5 15 F3
air Cl WR4 10 A2
akefield Gdns WR2 13 G1
akefield Rd WR2 13 G1
akefield Walk WR2 13 G1
akeney Cl WR5 14 D3
ake St WR5 15 E1
anquettes Av WR3 4 C6
anquettes St WR3 4 C6
enheim Rd WR2 7 G6
ockhouse Cl WR1 3 E3
oomfield Rd WR2 13 G2
ossom Cl WR5 9 H4
dium Cl WR4 10 A2
ilston Rd WR8 8 C6
mford Hill WR4 11 A5
rrowdale Dr WR4 9 G1
ughton Av WR2 13 F2
ughton Cl WR2 13 F1
ughton Park Cl WR2 13 G2
ughton St WR2 13 G2
urne St WR 8 B1
w Hill WR2 16 D5
wling Green Rd WR2 16 A1
wness Dr WR4 9 G1
zward St WR2 13 G1
adford Pl WR5 9 G5
amhope Cl WR4 9 G3
amley Av WR2 7 F2
amley Cl WR2 16 A2
amley Pl WR2 7 F2
ansford Rd WR2 13 E2
raymoor Rd,
Moor St WR1 8 B3
eam Cl WR5 14 C4
entwood Cl WR5 9 G6
ewery Walk WR1 8 B2
ickfields Rd WR4 9 E1
idge St WR1 3 B3
idgnorth Pl WR4 10 A2
ight Av WR4 11 B5
mstone Cl WR5 15 E4
ndley Rd WR4 5 H6
itannia Rd WR1 8 B3
tannia Sq WR1 8 B3
oad Walk WR1 3 C2
oadfield Cres WR3 5 F2
oadfield Gdns WR4 10 A3
oadmore Grn WR2 12 C2
oad St WR1 3 B2
oadway Gro WR2 13 E1
ockhampton Cl WR4 5 F5
ockweir WR3 9 E1
omich Rd WR2 13 H2
omsgrove St WR3 8 B1
omwich La WR2 13 H1
omwich Parade WR2 3 B3
omwich Parade WR5 14 B1
omwich Rd WR2 3 A1
omyard Rd WR2 13 F1
omyard Ter WR2 13 H1
onsil Cl WR5 15 G1
ookend La WR5 17 G3
ook Side WR5 17 G3
ookside Rd WR2 7 F5
ook St WR1 8 B1
ookthorpe Dr WR4 5 G6
oomhall WR5 15 F6
oomhall Grn WR5 15 E4
oomhall Way WR5 14 D5
oomhill La WR5 17 G1
oom Meadow Rd WR3 5 F2
owning Cl WR3 4 C6
own St WR2 13 H3
unswick Cl WR2 13 H4
ck St WR2 7 G6
ckholt Dr WR4 5 G5
cklewood WR3 8 D1
llfinch Cl WR5 14 D4
nns Rd WR5 14 D2
rdett Pl WR4 10 B4
rford Cl WR4 5 G5
rleigh Rd WR3 7 E6
rnham Cl WR5 14 D3
rnsall Cl WR5 9 G2
rtree Way WR4 10 B4
sh La WR2 16 B6

Butchers Walk WR3 5 G2
Buttermere Dr WR4 9 G1
Byefield Rise WR5 3 F2
Byron Cl WR2 16 A2

Caister Av WR4 10 B3
Calder Rd WR5 9 E4
Caldy Av WR5 15 F3
Calgary Dr WR2 13 G4
Camberwell Dr WR5 15 F4
Camden Pl WR1 8 C3
Camp Hill Av WR5 9 E6
Camp Hill Rd WR5 8 D6
Canada Way WR2 13 G3
Cangle La WR2 10 B3
Cannon St WR5 15 E1
Canterbury Rd WR5 9 F5
Carden Cl WR1 3 D3
Carden St WR1 3 D3
Carisbrooke Av WR4 10 B3
Carlisle Rd WR5 9 G5
Carriage Dr WR5 7 G5
Carrock Fell Av WR4 9 G1
Carters Cl WR4 9 F1
Cartmel Cl WR4 9 H1
Cartwright Av WR4 11 B5
Castell Pl WR4 10 A2
Castle Pl WR1 3 C4
Castle St WR1 3 B1
Catbrook WR3 9 E1
Catherine Rd WR2 13 G2
Cavendish St WR5 14 C1
Cecilia Av WR2 7 F3
Cecil Rd WR5 3 E3
Cedar Av WR4 9 F1
Celandine Dr WR5 14 D4
Chacewater Av WR3 4 A6
Chacewater Cres WR3 4 A6
Chadwick WR4 11 A5
Chalfont Cl WR3 4 B5
Chalford Dr WR4 5 G5
Chamberlain Rd WR2 13 G3
Chapel Rd WR5 17 F4
Chapel Walk WR1 3 C2
Charles St WR1 3 D3
Charnwood Cl WR2 13 G4
Charter Pl WR1 3 B1
Chase End Cl WR5 15 E2
Chatcombe Dr WR4 5 G6
Checketts Cl WR3 4 C5
Checketts La WR3 4 B5
Chedworth Dr WR4 5 G5
Chelmsford Dr WR5 9 F5
Chepstow Av WR4 10 A2
Chequers La WR2 3 A2
Cherington Cl WR4 5 F5
Cherry St WR5 14 D1
Cherry Tree Walk WR1 3 B1
Cherwell Cl WR4 9 F3
Cheshire Cheese Entry WR1 3 C1
Chester Cl WR5 9 G5
Chestnut Walk WR1 8 C3
Cheviot Cl WR4 9 F3
Chilham Pl WR4 10 B2
Chiltern Cl WR4 9 F3
Christchurch Rd WR4 9 E3
Christine Av WR2 12 D3
Church La,
Lower Broadheath WR2 6 B1
Church La,Tibberton WR9 10 F2
Church La, Norton WR5 15 H6
Church La,
Whittington WR5 15 H3
Church Rd WR2 13 H1
Church Rd WR3 8 D2
Church St WR1 3 C2
Church St, Kempsey WR5 17 F4
Cirencester Pl WR4 5 H5
City Arcade WR1 3 C3
City Walls Rd WR1 3 D3
Claines La WR3 4 C2
Claire St WR1 3 D3
Claphill La WR2 12 D1
Clarkson Gdns WR4 11 B5
Claverham Cl WR2 13 H2
Cleve Dr WR4 5 G6
Cobden Av WR4 11 B5
Coberley Cl WR4 5 G6

Cole Hill WR5 3 E4
Coleridge Cl WR3 8 C1
Colesborne Cl WR4 5 F6
Colin Rd WR3 4 B4
College Grn WR1 3 C4
College Precincts WR1 3 C4
College St WR1 3 D3
College Yard WR1 3 C3
Colletts Green Rd WR2 16 A1
Collings Av WR4 11 A5
Coltishall Cl WR5 15 E3
Columbia Dr WR2 13 F4
Comer Av WR2 7 G6
Comer Gdns WR2 7 F5
Comer Rd WR2 7 G5
Commandery Rd WR5 3 D4
Compton Rd WR5 3 F3
Conisborough WR4 10 B2
Coniston Cl WR4 9 G2
Connaught Cl WR5 14 D3
Constance Rd WR3 4 A4
Conway WR4 9 F3
Coombs Rd WR3 4 B6
Coopers Cl WR4 9 F1
Copenhagen St WR1 3 C3
Cope Rd WR3 4 C5
Copsewood Av WR4 9 H4
Copsewood Av WR5 9 H4
Corfe Av WR4 10 A3
Cormorant Rise WR2 13 H4
Cornmarket WR1 3 D2
Cornmeadow Grn WR3 4 B3
Cornmeadow La WR3 4 B4
Cosgrove Cl WR4 5 F5
Cotland WR3 8 D1
Cotswold Way WR4 5 G5
Courtland Rd WR3 4 B4
Coventry Av WR2 13 H3
Crane Dr WR2 13 H4
Cranesbill Dr WR5 14 D4
Cranham Dr WR4 5 F5
Cresswell Cl WR3 5 F2
Crickley Dr WR4 5 G6
Croft Rd WR 3 B2
Croft Walk WR1 3 B2
Cromwell Cres WR5 15 F1
Cromwell Cres La WR5 15 F1
Cromwell Rd WR2 16 A3
Cromwell St WR1 3 E2
Crookbarrow Way WR5 15 E4
Croome Rd WR2 13 G3
Crown Cl WR2 6 B2
Crown East La WR2 6 A4
Crown Meadow WR2 6 C2
Crown Passage WR1 3 C2
Crown St WR3 8 B1
Cumberland St WR1 8 B2
Cypress St WR3 4 C6
Cyril Rd WR3 8 D2

Dace Rd WR5 14 C4
Dalegarth Ct WR5 5 H6
Damaskfield WR4 10 A4
Danes Grn WR3 5 E1
Dart Rd WR5 9 F4
Daty Croft WR4 9 H3
Dawson Cl WR4 13 G4
Deal Cres WR4 10 B2
Deane Cl WR2 16 A3
Deansway WR1 3 C2
Debdale Av WR4 10 A3
Deer Av WR5 15 F3
Dee Way WR4 9 F3
Dent Cl WR5 3 E3
Derby Rd WR5 3 D4
Derwent Cl WR4 9 F1
Devon Rd WR5 9 F6
Diglis Av WR1 8 C6
Diglis Dock Rd WR5 14 B2
Diglis La WR5 14 C1
Diglis Rd WR5 8 C6
Dilmore Av WR3 5 E2
Dilmore La WR3 5 E2
Dilmore Rd WR5 5 F2
Dinchall WR5 15 H1
Dolday WR1 3 B2
Dolphin Cl WR2 7 G4
Don Rd WR4 9 F3

Dormouse Croft WR5 15 F3
Dorothy Cres WR3 4 B4
Dove Cl WR4 9 F3
Dover Av WR4 10 B2
Downlands Gdns WR2 7 F6
Dragonfly Grn WR5 15 F3
Drake Av WR2 7 E6
Drake Pl WR2 13 F1
Drapers Cl WR4 5 F6
Droitwich Rd WR3 4 C4
Drovers Way WR3 5 E6
Drumbles La WR4 10 A4
Dryden Cl WR3 4 C6
Duck Meadow WR4 9 H2
Dudley Cl WR2 7 E5
Dugdale Dr WR4 11 A5
Dunmow Av WR4 11 B6
Dunster Cl WR4 10 A2
Durham Rd WR5 9 G4
Dutton St WR3 8 D3

Eagle Cl WR5 14 D4
Earlsdon Rd WR2 13 G3
Eastbank Dr WR3 4 A5
East Comer WR2 7 G4
Eastfield Cl WR3 5 F2
Eastnor Cl WR5 15 F2
East St WR1 8 C3
Eastwood Rd WR 8 D2
Easy Row WR1 3 B1
Ebrington Dr WR4 5 H5
Edgar St WR1 3 D4
Edgeworth Cl WR4 5 G6
Edmonton Cl WR2 13 G4
Edward Cl WR5 3 F4
Egg La WR3 4 C1
Egremont Gdns WR4 10 B3
Elbury Park Rd WR4 9 G3
Elgar Dr WR5 17 G5
Eliot Rd WR3 4 C6
Elizabeth Av WR3 4 B4
Elkstone Cl WR4 5 F5
Ellison Av WR2 7 F3
Ellis Rd WR2 13 H2
Ellsdon WR5 17 G4
Ellsdon Rise WR5 17 G4
Elm Green Cl WR5 14 C3
Elmdale Rd WR3 4 B4
Elmfield Gdns WR5 8 D6
Elm Rd WR2 7 H5
Eltric Rd WR3 4 B4
Ely Cl WR5 9 G5
Emerald Rd WR2 7 F5
Emperor Dr WR5 15 F4
Ennerdale Dr WR4 9 G2
Epsom Cl WR3 5 F2
Eskdale Cl WR4 9 F2
Essex Cl WR2 7 E6
Evendine Cl WR5 15 E1
Everard Cl WR2 7 F3
Exbury Pl WR5 15 E3
Exeter Rd WR5 9 G4
Fairbairn Av WR3 4 B5
Fairfield Cl WR4 9 F1

Falcon Cl WR5 14 D4
Farley St WR2 7 F4
Farmbrook Cl WR2 13 E1
Farm Cl WR3 5 E6
Farne Av WR5 15 E3
Farnham Grn WR4 10 A2
Farrier St WR1 3 C1
Farundles Av WR4 10 A4
Ferndale Cl WR3 4 A4
Fern Rd WR2 7 G4
Ferry Bank WR2 7 G4
Ferry Cl WR2 7 G4
Field Cl WR3 5 E6
Fielden Row WR4 11 B6
Fieldhead Cl WR2 13 E1
Field Rd WR3 WR4 5 E6
Field Ter WR5 8 C6
Field Walk WR5 14 D2
Fir Tree Rd WR4 5 G2
Fir Way WR4 9 E1
First Av WR2 13 H3
Fish St WR1 3 C3
Fitcher Ct WR2 7 F2

ayfield Av WR3	8 D2
ayfield Rd WR3	8 D1
cCormick Av WR4	11 B5
clntyre Rd WR2	13 G1
cNaught Pl WR1	8 C3
eadowbank Dr WR2	13 E2
eadow Rd WR3	4 B3
ealcheapen St WR1	3 D2
edway Rd WR5	9 E4
elbourne St WR3	8 C1
elrose Cl WR2	7 G5
endip Cl WR4	9 F3
enston Cl WR4	9 G2
errimans Ct WR3	8 C2
errimans Hill Rd WR3	8 C2
errimans Walk WR3	8 C2
ersey Rd WR5	9 E4
erton Cl WR4	9 E3
iddle Hollow Dr WR4	9 G2
iddle Rd WR2	13 G2
iddles Av WR4	9 H2
iddle St WR1	3 D1
iddleton Gdns WR4	9 H1
idhurst Cl WR5	9 E6
idland Rd WR4 WR5	3 F3
illbrook Cl WR3	4 A5
illers Cl WR4	9 F1
illhams Av WR4	10 A3
ill Wood Dr WR4	9 H3
ilret Cl WR3	8 C2
inett Av WR2	12 D3
oat House La WR3	5 E4
onarch Dr WR2	7 F3
onarch Pl WR2	7 F3
ontgomerie Cl WR2	16 A3
ontreal Cl WR2	13 G4
oor St WR1	8 B3
orrin Cl WR3	4 C4
orris Av WR3	4 B5
ortlake Av WR5	9 F6
orton Av WR3	5 E2
orton Pl WR1	3 B2
orton Rd WR3	5 E2
ailsworth Cl WR4	5 F6
apleton La WR5	17 G5
arrow Walk WR2	13 G1
ash Cl WR3	4 B3
ashs Passage WR1	3 D3
avigation Rd WR5	14 C1
eason Rd WR4	11 A5
elson Rd WR2	13 G1
ew Bank St WR3	8 B1
ewbury Rd WR2	7 F5
eweys Hill WR3	4 A6
ewland Cres WR2	13 E2
ewport St WR1	3 B2
ew Rd WR2	3 A3
ew St WR1	3 D3
ewtown Rd WR5	3 F2
ewtown St WR5	9 E4
bley Cl WR4	5 F6
ghtingale Av WR4	11 A6
ne Acres Grn WR4	9 H3
xon Ct WR2	16 D5
orfolk Cl WR2	7 E5
orham Pl WR4	9 H1
orham Pl WR4	10 A3
orth Croft WR2	13 G2
orthbrook Cl WR3	8 C1
orthcote St WR3	8 B1
orthfield Cl WR3	5 F2
orthfield La WR2	16 B6
orthfield St WR1	8 C3
orthleach Cl WR4	5 F5
orth Parade WR1	3 B2
orth Quay WR1	3 B2
orthwick Av WR3	4 B6
orthwick Cl WR3	4 A5
orthwick Rd WR3	4 A2
orthwick Wlk WR3	4 B6
orthwood Cl WR	8 C1
orton Cl WR4	14 C3
orton Rd WR5	14 D3
orton Rd WR5	15 E4
orwich Rd WR5	9 F5
uffield Cl WR2	7 F5
unnery La WR5	9 F6
Nunnery Way WR5	11 A7
Nursery Rd WR2	13 G2
Oak Av WR4	9 E1
Oakfield Dr WR5	17 G5
Oaklands WR4	9 H4
Oakridge Cl WR4	5 H6
Oakville Cl WR2	13 G4
Offerton La WR3	10 C1
Offley St WR3	8 C1
Ogilvy Sq WR3	4 B5
O'Keys La WR3	5 G2
Oldbury Rd WR2	7 E5
Old Malvern Rd WR2	16 A2
Old Northwick La WR3	4 A4
Old Rd WR2	13 G5
Old Rd WR5	17 F6
Old Rd North WR5	17 F4
Old Rd South WR5	17 F6
Old Rectory Cl WR2	16 C1
Ombersley Rd WR3	4 B4
Ontario Cl WR2	13 G5
Orchard Cl WR2	12 D3
Orchard St WR5	14 C2
Orchard Way WR2	16 D5
Orchid Cl WR5	14 D5
Oriel Cl WR4	9 E3
Orwin Dr WR4	11 A5
Osier Cl WR5	14 D2
Osprey Cl WR2	13 H4
Otherton La WR6	12 A2
Otley Cl WR4	9 G3
Ottawa Cl WR2	13 G4
Otter La WR5	15 F3
Overthwart Cres WR4	10 A4
Oxford Cl WR5	9 F5
Packington WR2	7 G3
Padmore St WR1	3 E1
Painswick Cl WR4	5 G6
Palmers Grn WR2	13 G2
Park Av WR3	8 A1
Parkfield La WR2	7 F2
Parkland Rd WR3	4 A3
Park La, Hallow WR2	7 E1
Park La WR3	8 B1
Park St WR5	3 E3
Park View Ter WR3	4 A6
Parsonage Way WR4	10 C4
Partridge Cl WR5	14 D4
Partridge La WR2	6 B2
Patterdale Dr WR4	9 G1
Peabody Av WR4	11 A5
Peachley Gdns WR2	6 B1
Peachley La WR2	6 B1
Peacock Cl WR5	15 E4
Penbury St WR3	4 B6
Penhill Cres WR2	7 F6
Penmanor Cl WR2	7 F6
Penrith Cl WR4	9 H1
Perch Rd WR5	14 C4
Perdiswell St WR3	4 B6
Permain Cl WR2	7 F2
Perrywood Cl WR5	9 E6
Perrywood Wlk WR5	9 E6
Pershore La WR4	10 C1
Peterborough Cl WR5	9 F4
Petunnia Cl WR5	14 D4
Pevensey Cl WR5	15 E1
Pheasant St WR1	3 D1
Philip Rd WR3	4 B4
Pickering Grn WR4	10 B3
Pierpoint St WR1	3 C1
Pine Cl WR3	5 G2
Pine Way WR4	5 E6
Pinkett St WR3	4 B5
Pinkus Cl WR4	11 A5
Pippen Field WR4	10 B4
Pirie Av WR4	11 B5
Pitchcroft La WR1	8 A1
Pitmaston Rd WR2	13 G2
Pitt Av WR4	11 A5
Pixham Ferry La, Callow End WR2	16 C6
Pixham Ferry La, Kempsey WR5	17 E6
Plantation Dr WR4	10 A3
Plough Croft WR4	9 H2
Ploughmans Cl WR4	9 F1
Plough Rd WR9	10 F1
Pole Elm Cl WR2	16 D4
Pope Iron Rd WR1	8 A1
Poplar Av WR4	9 E1
Portefields Rd WR4	9 F3
Portland St WR1	8 C6
Portland Walk WR1	8 C6
Portsmouth Cl WR5	9 G5
Post Office La, Fernhill Heath WR3	5 G1
Post Office La, Kempsey WR5	17 G4
Potters Cl WR4	9 F1
Pound Walk WR1	8 A2
Powderham Av WR4	10 B3
Powells Row WR2	13 H1
Powick Walk WR1	3 C2
Powyke Court Cl WR2	16 C1
Prescott Dr WR4	5 G5
Prestbury Cl WR4	5 F6
Prestwich Av WR5	9 F6
Price St WR3	8 C1
Primrose Cres WR5	14 D4
Prince Rupert Av WR2	16 A2
Prince Rupert St WR5	3 D3
Priory Rd WR2	13 G3
Prospect Pl WR5	8 D6
Providence St WR1	3 D3
Pump St WR1	3 C3
Purleigh Av WR4	10 B3
Quay St WR1	3 B2
Quebec Cl WR2	13 F4
Queen St WR1	3 D2
Queenswood Dr WR5	15 E3
Quisters WR4	10 A4
Race Field WR4	10 A3
Radnor Croft WR3	5 E5
Raglan St WR3	8 B1
Railway Walk WR3	8 D3
Rainbow Hill WR3	8 D3
Rainbow Hill Ter WR3	8 D3
Rainthorpe Av WR5	15 E3
Raleigh Cl WR2	7 E6
Randwick Cl WR4	5 F6
Randwick Dr WR4	5 F6
Rannoch Av WR5	15 E3
Ransom Av WR5	14 D2
Raven Dr WR5	14 D4
Ravenshill Cl WR5	15 E3
Rea Way WR2	13 F1
Rectory Cl WR2	6 B1
Rectory Gdns WR2	7 H6
Redcliffe St WR3	4 A6
Redfern Av WR5	9 F6
Red Hill La WR5	15 F1
Reedham Cl WR3	4 A5
Regiment Cl WR5	15 F5
Regina Cl WR2	13 G4
Reindeer Ct WR1	3 D2
Reservoir La WR3	8 D3
Ribble Cl WR5	9 E5
Ribston Cl WR2	7 F3
Richmond Hill WR5	3 E3
Richmond Rd WR5	3 E4
Ripon Rd WR5	9 G4
Riverview Cl WR2	7 G3
Roach Cl WR5	14 D4
Robert Owen Ct WR1	3 E2
Robin Cl WR5	14 D4
Rodborough Cl WR4	5 G5
Rodborough Dr WR4	5 G5
Rogers Hill WR3	8 D2
Ronkswood Cres WR5	9 E4
Ronkswood Hill WR4	9 E4
Rose Av WR4	9 E3
Rosemary Av WR2	13 F1
Rosemoor Gdns WR5	15 E3
Rose Ter WR5	3 E4
Rough Meadow WR4	9 H2
Roundtree Grn WR4	11 B6
Rowan Av WR4	9 E3
Rowley Hill St WR2	7 G6
Russell Cl WR2	16 A2
Russet Cl WR2	7 F3
Rydal Cl WR4	9 F2
Ryland Cl WR3	5 E5
Sabrina Av WR3	4 B6
Sabrina Ter WR1	8 B2
Sabrina Wlk WR3	4 B6
St Albans Cl WR5	9 F4
St Annes Cl WR3	4 C4
St Annes Rd WR3	4 B4
St Audries Rd WR5	14 D1
St Catherines Hill WR5	3 F4
St Catherines Vale WR5	9 E6
St Clements Cl WR2	3 A3
St Clements Ct WR2	3 A3
St Clements Gdns WR2	3 A3
St Dunstans Cl WR5	14 D1
St Dunstans Cres WR5	8 D6
St Egwine Cl WR3	8 C2
St Georges La North WR1	8 B2
St Georges La South WR1	8 B2
St Georges Sq WR1	8 B2
St Georges Walk WR1	8 B2
St Johns Cl WR3	4 C4
St Lawrence Cl WR2	13 G4
St Marks Cl WR5	14 D2
St Martins Gate WR	3 D2
St Martins Walk WR1	3 E2
St Marys St WR1	8 C3
St Michaels Rd WR3	4 C4
St Moritz Cl WR3	4 A4
St Nicholas St WR1	3 C2
St Oswalds Rd WR	8 C3
St Pauls St WR1	3 E3
St Pauls Walk WR1	3 E2
St Peters Dr WR5	14 D4
St Peters Hill WR5	14 C4
St Peters St WR1	3 D4
St Stephens St WR3	4 B6
St Swithins St WR1	3 C2
St Swithuns Cl WR5	8 D6
St Wulstans Cres WR5	3 E4
Salisbury Cl WR5	9 F6
Salisbury Cl WR5	9 G5
Salters Cl WR4	5 F6
Saltwood Av WR4	10 A3
Sanctuary Cl WR2	7 F6
Sandpiper Cl WR5	15 E3
Sandys Rd WR1	8 A1
Sansome Fields Walk WR1	8 C3
Sansome Mews WR1	8 C3
Sansome Pl WR1	3 C1
Sansome St WR1	3 C2
Sansome Walk WR1	3 C1
Sapphire Cres WR2	7 F6
Saunders St WR3	4 B5
Scaffell Cl WR4	9 G2
School Rd WR2	13 G1
School Walk WR5	15 H3
Seathwaite Pl WR4	9 G1
Sebright Av WR5	9 E6
Sedge Cl WR2	13 F1
Selbourne Rd WR1	8 B2
Selbourne Rd West WR1	8 B2
Selsey Cl WR4	5 G6
Seven Acres WR4	9 H2
Severn Grange WR3	4 A3
Severn St WR1	3 C4
Severn Ter WR1	3 A1
Seymour Av WR3	4 B5
Shakespeare Rd WR2	7 E6
Shap Dr WR4	9 G1
Sharman Cl WR1	8 B2
Sharman Rd WR1	8 B2
Sharpe Rd WR2	13 H3
Shaw St WR1	3 C2
Sheepscombe Dr WR4	5 G6
Sheffield Cl WR5	9 G6
Sheldon Park Rd WR3	4 A3
Shelley Cl WR3	4 C6
Sheringham Rd WR5	14 D3
Sherriff St WR4	9 E4
Sherwood La WR2	13 G4
Shetland Cl WR3	5 E5
Shipstow Cl WR	5 F5
Shipwrights Cl WR4	5 F6
Shrawley Rd WR3	5 F2
Shrubbery Av WR1	8 B2
Shrubbery Rd WR1	8 C2
Shrub Hill WR1	3 F1

Edition 567 A 9.9